Distinctive Doctrines of the Apostolic Church:
An Apostolic Pentecostal Perspective on Foundational Bible Doctrines

By Kelly Nix

Distinctive Doctrines of the Apostolic Church
By Kelly Nix

©2015, Kelly Nix
San Antonio, Texas 78250

All rights reserved. No portion of this publication may be reproduced, stored in an electronic system, or transmitted in any form or by any means, electronic, mechanical, photocopy, recording, or otherwise, without the prior permission of Kelly Nix. Brief quotations may be used in literary review.

ISBN-13: 978-1507541098
ISBN-10: 1507541090

Preface

This book is the result of many years of teaching core Apostolic doctrine to the congregations to which I've ministered, as well as to my students in Bible college. It is intended to introduce the reader at a very basic level to teachings of the Apostolic church that I consider to be distinctive and essential, while creating an appetite for deeper knowledge of the Scriptures. Other key Apostolic doctrines such as the Oneness of God, spiritual gifts and a lifestyle of holiness and separation unto the Lord will be dealt with in a subsequent book. Appendices are also provided for those who wish to study some subjects in a little more depth.

Contents

Preface 3
Chapter 1: God 7
   God is the Creator 8
   The Attributes of God 11
   The Word of God 13
Chapter 2: Faith 17
   The Faith that Pleases God 19
   Faith Puts God in Action 21
   Faith and Grace 22
   Inward Faith...Outward Obedience 24
   Building Faith 28
Chapter 3: Repentance 29
   What is Sin? 30
   The Call to Repentance 31
   The Meaning of "Repentance" 34
   Total Separation from the World 36
   A Repented Heart Makes Restitution 39
Chapter 4: Water Baptism 43
   The Necessity of Water Baptism 45
   The Purpose of Water Baptism 46
   The Biblical Method of Baptism 48
   Who May Be Baptized? 50

    What Is the Proper Baptismal Formula?............ 52
    Do I Need to be Rebaptized? 58
Chapter 5: The Baptism of the Holy Ghost 61
    What is the Gift of the Holy Ghost? 62
    The Purpose of the Gift of the Holy Ghost 63
    Receiving the Gift of the Holy Ghost 66
    The Sign of Receiving the Gift of the Holy Ghost 68
Conclusion 75
Appendix A 77
Appendix B 91

Distinctive Doctrines of the Apostolic Church:
An Apostolic Pentecostal Perspective on Foundational Bible Doctrines

By Kelly Nix

Chapter 1: God

The Bible, God's Word, is a fascinating book. It carries us back to the very beginning of the universe, describes to us in detail its creation, and then launches us into a compelling account of the history of man and the development of civilization. It presents us with a legal system upon which mankind has never been able to improve, introduces us to beautiful oriental prose and poetry, and presents us with amazingly detailed genealogical records. It carries us into kings' courts and teaches us civics. It also presents to us, in language simple enough for a child to understand, a foolproof set of instructions on how to find salvation and deliverance from sin.

There is one thing, however, the Bible does ***not*** do: it never attempts to prove the existence of God. Why? Simply because it advances on the principle that only a fool could look at the wonders of nature all around us and doubt that God exists.

> *"The fool hath said in his heart, There is no God" (Psalm 14:1).*
> *"Because that which may be known of God is manifest in them; for God hath shewed it unto them. For the invisible things of him from the*

creation of the world are clearly seen, being understood by the things that are made, even his eternal power and Godhead; so that they are without excuse" (Romans 1:19-20).

That's why, instead of launching into an argument on the existence of God, the Bible simply begins its great account by saying,

"In the beginning God created the heaven and the earth" (Genesis 1:1).

Before a man or a woman can successfully approach God, he or she must be fully convinced of the following two things: 1) God exists, and 2) He will reward those who earnestly seek Him. If you look for Him, He will allow Himself to be found!

"But without faith it is impossible to please him: for he that cometh to God must believe that he is, and that he is a rewarder of them that diligently seek him" (Hebrews 11:6).
"Draw nigh to God, and he will draw nigh to you...." (James 4:8).

God is the Creator

The theory of evolution asserts that the world (and the whole universe) is not the result of a creative act by God (in fact, it denies the existence of God), but rather the result of a set of accidental circumstances. While the purpose of this lesson is not to go into a scientific discussion of creation versus evolution, suffice it to say that the mathematical probability of any one of the many "accidents" required to validate the theory of evolution actually happening is not even remotely possible. The Word of God declares that the universe and everything in it is the result of God's conscious design and handiwork.

> *"For the Lord is a great God, and a great King above all gods. In his hand are the deep places of the earth: the strength of the hills is his also. The sea is his, and he made it: and his hands formed the dry land" (Psalm 95:3-5).*
>
> *"Through faith we understand that the worlds were framed by the word of God, so that things which are seen were not made of things which do appear" (Hebrews 11:3).*

Ask yourself this question: What are the chances that, should all of the different gears, springs, and parts already *happen* to have spontaneously come into existence, being of *precisely* the proper measurements, if you were to take all of these parts, place them in a jar, and shake them vigorously, they would by themselves unite into a working wristwatch, already set to the proper time? Even if you should attempt this process **millions of times over**, the chance of a working wristwatch being born of parts randomly shaken together is **less than nonexistent**. And yet, the theory of evolution, which teaches that this is precisely the type of process that brought the universe into existence, is called a "science", and the Biblical teaching of an intelligent Creator is dismissed as fiction….

> *"Because that, when they knew God, they glorified him not as God, neither were thankful; but became vain in their imaginations, and their foolish heart was darkened. Professing themselves to be wise, they became fools…." (Romans 1:21-22).*

This book is not written to attempt to convince the skeptic that God is real. Instead, it assumes the reader accepts the existence of God as fact and the Word of God as truth. The Bible declares that God is the sole Creator of the universe; no other god existed or was present with Him at creation.

> *"Thus saith the Lord, thy redeemer, and he that formed thee from the womb, I am the Lord that maketh all things; that stretcheth forth the heavens alone; that spreadeth abroad the earth by myself" (Isaiah 44:24).*

"For thus saith the Lord that created the heavens; God himself that formed the earth and made it; he hath established it, he created it not in vain, he formed it to be inhabited: I am the Lord; and there is none else" (Isaiah 45:18).

Everything that exists – be it plant, animal, mineral, or human – is the handiwork of God. He made it all by Himself, and He made it for His pleasure – to do His will.

"Thou art worthy, O Lord, to receive glory and honour and power: for thou hast created all things, and for thy pleasure they are and were created." (Revelation 4:11).

The Attributes of God

God possesses a number of attributes or qualities that, together, make Him what He is. In his book *The Oneness of God*, Dr. David Bernard mentions the following *personal* attributes of God:[1]

1. God is a *Spirit* (John 4:24)
2. God is *invisible* (I Timothy 1:17)
3. God is *omnipresent*, or present everywhere (Acts 17:27-28)

---

[1] Bernard, D. (1983). The Nature of God. In *The nature of God* (pp. 23-32). Hazelwood, Mo.: Word Aflame Press.

4. God is *omniscient*, or knows all things (Job 42:2)
5. God is *omnipotent*, or has all power (Revelation 19:6)
6. God is *eternal*, meaning He has no beginning or ending (Revelation 1:8)
7. God is *immutable*, or unchanging (Malachi 3:6)

Dr. Bernard goes on to list what he refers to as God's *moral* attributes:
1. Love (I John 4:8)
2. Light (I John 1:5)
3. Holiness (I Peter 1:16)
4. Mercy (Psalm 103:8)
5. Gentleness (Psalm 18:35)
6. Righteousness (Psalm 129:4)
7. Goodness (Romans 2:4)
8. Perfection (Matthew 5:48)
9. Justice (Isaiah 45:21)
10. Faithfulness (I Corinthians 10:13)
11. Truth (John 17:17)
12. Grace (Psalm 103:8)

Because of our limitations as mortal, created human beings, we can never possess God's personal attributes. But the beautiful thing is that we *can* reflect His moral attributes! By establishing a relationship with Him and being born of His Spirit (a process we'll discuss in a later chapter), we become more and more like our Creator. For example, the same passage of Scripture that declares the holiness of God invites us to share in that attribute:

> *"But as he which hath called you is holy, so be ye holy in all manner of conversation; because it is written, Be ye holy; for I am holy" (I Peter 1:15-16).*

Likewise, the Apostle John instructs us that we should love one another because love is of God, and Paul tells us that the love of God is poured into our hearts by God's Spirit.

> *"Beloved, let us love one another: for love is of God; and every one that loveth is born of God, and knoweth God" (I John 4:7).*
> *"And hope maketh not ashamed; because the love of God is shed abroad in our hearts by the Holy Ghost which is given unto us" (Romans 5:5).*

The Word of God

It would not be proper to close out this chapter without taking a brief look at the means by which God has chosen to communicate with humanity. His thoughts, commandments, counsel, and instructions are delivered to us through the pages of His Word, the Bible.

The Bible is actually a collection of different books – 66 in all. These 66 books were written by different men, and most of them never knew each other. The Bible covers over 4,000 years of the history of the world, and also provides prophetic insight into our day and beyond. It has two major divisions: the Old Testament and the New Testament. The Old Testament has 39 books, and the New Testament has 27. Between the Old and New Testaments are 400 years commonly referred to as the "400 years of silence" because we have no record of God speaking to man during that period.

Books of the Old Testament

Genesis	II Chronicles	Daniel
Exodus	Ezra	Hosea
Leviticus	Nehemiah	Joel
Numbers	Esther	Amos
Deuteronomy	Job	Obadiah
Joshua	Psalms	Jonah
Judges	Proverbs	Micah
Ruth	Ecclesiastes	Nahum
I Samuel	Song of Solomon	Habakkuk
II Samuel	Isaiah	Zephaniah
I Kings	Jeremiah	Haggai
II Kings	Lamentations	Zechariah
I Chronicles	Ezekiel	Malachi

Books of the New Testament

Matthew	Ephesians	Hebrews
Mark	Philippians	James
Luke	Colossians	I Peter
John	I Thessalonians	II Peter
Acts	II Thessalonians	I John
Romans	I Timothy	II John
I Corinthians	II Timothy	III John
II Corinthians	Titus	Jude
Galatians	Philemon	Revelation

The Old Testament consists of five major divisions: Law (Genesis – Deuteronomy), History (Joshua – Esther), Poetry (Job – Song of Solomon), Major Prophets (Isaiah – Daniel), and Minor Prophets (Hosea – Malachi). The terms "Major Prophets" and "Minor Prophets" have nothing to do with the importance of the writers, but simply refer to the size of the books they wrote.

The New Testament has four major divisions: the Books of the Gospel (Matthew – John), History (Acts), the Epistles (Romans – Jude), and Prophecy (Revelation). The Epistles are letters written to the church by the apostles.

Even though these books had many writers, they have only one author – God Himself. According to the Bible, the Scriptures are inspired by God, and are not to be interpreted to suit our own desires. They are His Word, and must be interpreted in the light of His nature, His identity, His will, and His purpose.

> "All scripture is given by inspiration of God, and is profitable for doctrine, for reproof, for correction, for instruction in righteousness" (II Timothy 3:16).
>
> "We have also a more sure word of prophecy; whereunto ye do well that ye take heed, as unto a light that shineth in a dark place, until the day dawn, and the day star arise in your hearts: Knowing this first, that no prophecy of the scripture is of any private interpretation. For the prophecy came not in old time by the will of man: but holy men of God spake as they were moved by the Holy Ghost" (II Peter 1:19-21).

Chapter 2: Faith

Faith is essential to your walk with God. In fact, the Bible goes so far as to say that, if you don't have faith, you can't even please God! Clearly, if faith is so important, we need to be certain we have a clear understanding of what faith really is.

Hebrews 11:1 gives us a good definition of faith. It says faith is two things: the *substance* of things hoped for, and the *evidence* of things not seen.

> *"Now faith is the substance of things hoped for, the evidence of things not seen"* (Hebrews 11:1).

Let's take a look at the meanings of these words. The definitions of "substance" include (among others): 1. essential nature, 2. a fundamental or characteristic part or quality, 3. ultimate reality that underlies all outward manifestations and change, and 4. physical material from which something is made or which has discrete existence.[2] From all this complicated language, the basic truth we need to learn is that faith is something **solid**. Even though it can't be touched or handled, faith is real.

---

[2] Substance. (n.d.). Retrieved January 12, 2015, from http://www.merriam-webster.com/dictionary/substance.

The same source tells us that the word "evidence" means, among other things: 1. an outward sign, 2. something that furnishes proof, and 3. one who bears witness. In other words, this means faith is ***indisputable***.

Now we begin to see what a mighty force faith is. When we have real faith in God, even though we don't yet see what He will do, we still consider His promises to be fact – something solid and indisputable. The things we hope for and the things we don't yet see are, to us, just as real as if we had them in our hands. We have no doubt that God will do just as He said. This is the kind of trust God rewards!

Remember, it is impossible to please God without faith. Perhaps you are thinking, "I could never have the kind of faith it takes to please God!" Don't despair! The Bible assures us that God has given to each of us a measure of faith.

"...God hath dealt to every man the measure of faith" (Romans 12:3)

Therefore, since God has already provided you with a measure of faith, it is your responsibility to develop it, nurture it, and exercise it.

The Faith that Pleases God

All too often, we refuse to believe anything we have not seen for ourselves. While this may be a wise practice in matters of this world, it will not work in our dealings with God. The faith God accepts from us is a blind faith – the simple, undoubting faith of a small child. If we want to please God, we must believe that God's promises are true, even when we don't see an immediate result. Consider the example of the Roman centurion, who refused to bring Jesus to his home, believing instead that all Jesus had to do was speak the word right where He was, and his servant would be healed:

> "The centurion answered and said, Lord, I am not worthy that thou shouldest come under my roof: but speak the word only, and my servant shall be healed. For I am a man under authority, having soldiers under me: and I say to this man, Go, and he goeth; and to another, Come, and he cometh; and to my servant, Do this, and he doeth it. When Jesus heard it, he marvelled, and said to them that followed, Verily I say unto you, I have not found so great faith, no, not in Israel…And Jesus said unto the centurion, Go thy way; and as thou hast believed, so be it done unto thee. And his servant was healed in the selfsame hour" (Matthew 8:8-10; 13).

Consider the words Jesus spoke to Thomas:

"Jesus saith unto him, Thomas, because thou hast seen me, thou hast believed: blessed are they that have not seen, and yet have believed" (John 20:29).

It is hard to imagine God being impressed by anything. All He had to do was speak the word, and the universe came into existence! When He wanted His people to pass through the Red Sea on dry ground, He simply blew on the waters and they opened. He sent fire from heaven on a number of occasions. So what could a mere human being do to impress such a God?

The answer is simpler than you might think. God has a soft spot in His heart for faith! If you simply believe Him without doubting, you will make a powerful impression on God. There is nothing that hurts Him more than for someone to doubt His word, and there is nothing that pleases Him more than for someone to believe it!

"Then Jesus answered and said unto her, O woman, great is thy faith: be it unto thee even as thou wilt. And her daughter was made whole from that very hour" (Matthew 15:28).

Faith Puts God in Action

If you want to discover how to put God in action, use your faith! Nothing gets Him to respond more effectively than faith. Notice how Jesus replied to the woman who reached out to Him for healing:

> "But Jesus turned him about, and when he saw her, he said, Daughter, be of good comfort; thy faith hath made thee whole. And the woman was made whole from that hour" (Matthew 9:22).

Another good example of the way faith encourages God to move is the story of Bartimaeus. He put aside personal pride, embarrassment, and all other hindering factors and cried out to Jesus in faith. Once again, his faith captivated Jesus' attention, and he received his healing.

> "And Jesus said unto him, Go thy way; thy faith hath made thee whole. And immediately he received his sight, and followed Jesus in the way" (Mark 10:52).

The same is true of the sinful woman Luke wrote about:

"And he said to the woman, Thy faith hath saved thee; go in peace" (Luke 7:50).

One critical fact to remember is that, in order for faith to be effective, it must be expressed. God responds to our expression of faith. In Mark 2:5, it specifically says, "When Jesus **saw** their faith." In fact, the results of our prayers are determined by the level of our faith.

"Then touched he their eyes, saying, According to your faith be it unto you" (Matthew 9:29).

Lest you be left with the wrong impression, let me point out that God does not expect us to possess "super faith." Rather, we should realize that He will give us enough faith to believe for what needs to be done, because *it is His will to do it*.

"… For verily I say unto you, If ye have faith as a grain of mustard seed, ye shall say unto this mountain, Remove hence to yonder place; and it shall remove; and nothing shall be impossible unto you" (Matthew 17:20).

Faith and Grace

Let's think for a moment about how faith affects our salvation. Many people are confused about salvation by faith. Before we address this issue, however, let's make sure we have a clear understanding of the roles of faith and grace in justifying us from our sins.

The following verses show us how faith and grace work together. We are saved by the grace of God (the unmerited favor of God towards men), but we can only enter into that grace by faith. Therefore, faith and grace are mutually dependent; one does no good without the other.

> *"Being justified freely by his grace through the redemption that is in Christ Jesus: whom God hath set forth to be a propitiation through faith in his blood, to declare his righteousness for the remission of sins that are past, through the forbearance of God; to declare, I say, at this time his righteousness: that he might be just, and the justifier of him which believeth in Jesus. Where is boasting then? It is excluded. By what law? of works? Nay: but by the law of faith. Therefore we conclude that a man is justified by faith without the deeds of the law" (Romans 3:24-28).*
>
> *"Therefore being justified by faith, we have peace with God through our Lord Jesus Christ: by whom also we have access by faith into this grace wherein we stand, and rejoice in hope of the glory of God" (Romans 5:1-2).*

"For <u>by grace are ye saved through faith</u>; and that not of yourselves: it is the gift of God: not of works, lest any man should boast" (Ephesians 2:8-9).

Now that we have established biblically that salvation is by faith through grace, let's take a closer look at the role faith plays in our salvation. It is safe to say that the vast majority of people in most of the major denominations of Christianity do not fully understand this topic; and because of this, many are basing their salvation on an unsure foundation. We must be certain that our salvation experience exactly matches the Bible plan of salvation, because a mistake in this area could have eternal consequences!

Inward Faith...Outward Obedience

Many Christian denominations today teach that salvation is obtained merely by professing your faith in Jesus as your Savior, "accepting the Lord as your personal Savior" or "receiving Christ." Some even go so far as to say that such things as being water baptized or receiving the gift of the Holy Ghost are "works," and therefore are not a part of salvation. This is based on a very irresponsible interpretation of Ephesians 2:8-9, which we quoted above.

One of the most valuable principles of *hermeneutics* (the art and science of Biblical interpretation) is summed up in the old saying that *a text without a context is nothing but a pretext*. The "context" could be defined as what else the Bible has to say about a particular subject. If we take an individual verse of Scripture by itself without bothering to compare it to the rest of what the Bible has to say about that matter, it is easy to create erroneous doctrines. Remember that the whole truth about a subject is not always contained in a single verse or passage; sometimes pieces of the puzzle are spread all through the Bible, and God expects us to diligently search them out and put them together before formulating any doctrines.

In the case of salvation, many have seized on "for by grace are ye saved through faith" without seriously considering what faith really is. While Paul went on to say that we are not saved by works, the context of that scripture clearly indicates that he was referring to the ceremonial works of the Law of Moses. To say there is nothing we have to do in order to be saved is a direct contradiction of the Scripture, because the Apostle James wrote that faith without works is dead. In other words, if you really have faith, this will be demonstrated by your obedience to the Word of God. The works James is talking about are not works of the Mosaic Law, but works of obedience to God.

"Even so faith, if it hath not works, is dead, being alone. Yea, a man may say, Thou hast faith, and I have works: shew me thy faith without thy works, and I will shew thee my faith by my works. Thou believest that there is one God; thou doest well: the devils also believe, and tremble. But wilt thou know, O vain man, that faith without works is dead? Was not Abraham our father justified by works, when he had offered Isaac his son upon the altar? Seest thou how faith wrought with his works, and by works was faith made perfect? And the scripture was fulfilled which saith, Abraham believed God, and it was imputed unto him for righteousness: and he was called the Friend of God. Ye see then how that by works a man is justified, and not by faith only. Likewise also was not Rahab the harlot justified by works, when she had received the messengers, and had sent them out another way? For as the body without the spirit is dead, so faith without works is dead also" (James 2:17-26).

It's clear, then, that when Paul wrote that we are saved by grace through faith he was not simply speaking of making a verbal confession. True faith will be validated by our actions. If we do not obey the Word of God, we are demonstrating that we do not really believe it.

In fact, Jesus made it plain that salvation involves believing and obeying – not simply *professing* faith:

> *"He that believeth **and** is baptized shall be saved; but he that believeth not shall be damned" (Mark 16:16).*

He also condemned those who make verbal professions of faith, yet do not experience a change in their hearts and lives.

> *"This people draweth nigh unto me with their mouth, and honoureth me with their lips; but their heart is far from me. But in vain they do worship me, teaching for doctrines the commandments of men" (Matthew 15:8-9).*

Hide these scriptures in your heart, and spend time meditating on what they have to say about faith and salvation:

> *"He that believeth and is baptized shall be saved; but he that believeth not shall be damned" (Mark 16:16).*
> *"For God so loved the world, that he gave his only begotten Son, that whosoever believeth in him should not perish, but have everlasting life" (John 3:16).*

> *"And they said, Believe on the Lord Jesus Christ, and thou shalt be saved, and thy house" (Acts 16:31).*
>
> *"That if thou shalt confess with thy mouth the Lord Jesus, and shalt believe in thine heart that God hath raised him from the dead, thou shalt be saved. For with the heart man believeth unto righteousness; and with the mouth confession is made unto salvation" (Romans 10:9-10).*

Building Faith

Faith is the key to approaching God. Without it, you cannot please Him. He has provided every person with a basic measure of faith; but what can we do to increase it?

Perhaps the easiest way to obtain greater faith is to simply ask God for it. As you pray and read His Word, you'll find your faith growing. Ask him to give you more faith – He will!

> *"Jesus said unto him, If thou canst believe, all things are possible to him that believeth. And straightway the father of the child cried out, and said with tears, Lord, I believe; help thou mine unbelief" (Mark 9:23-24).*

Chapter 3: Repentance

Repentance is a difficult subject to approach. This is because it attacks many things we hold dear: our self-image, our pride, our ego. We have been conditioned to develop a high self-esteem and sense of personal worth. While these things have their proper place, they must be kept in a godly perspective. The Bible declares that all have sinned. Yes, **all**. Regardless of your upbringing, your good moral qualities, how upstanding a citizen you may be or how devout you are in your religious practices, if you are human, the Bible still says you are a sinner in God's sight.

As we pointed out in the previous chapter, we cannot even approach God without faith. However, when we do approach God, we must approach Him according to His terms and not ours. *Repentance* is right at the top of His list of priorities, and if we truly have faith, we will have to deal with it.

Let's look at the following Biblical proofs of the sinfulness of man:

"The fool hath said in his heart, There is no God. They are corrupt, they have done abominable works, there is none that doeth good. The Lord looked down from heaven upon the children of men, to see if there were any that did understand, and seek God. They are all gone aside, they are all together become filthy: there is none that doeth good, no, not one" (Psalm 14:1-3).

"For there is not a just man upon earth, that doeth good, and sinneth not" (Ecclesiastes 7:20).

"As it is written, There is none righteous, no, not one: there is none that understandeth, there is none that seeketh after God. They are all gone out of the way, they are together become unprofitable; there is none that doeth good, no, not one" (Romans 3:10-12).

"For all have sinned, and come short of the glory of God" (Romans 3:23).

"If we say that we have no sin, we deceive ourselves, and the truth is not in us…If we say that we have not sinned, we make him a liar, and his word is not in us" (I John 1:8, 10).

What is Sin?

Before we can discuss repentance, we first need to talk about *why* we need to repent in the first place. We read in the verses above that "all have sinned" and that "if we say we have not sinned, we make him a liar." What does it mean when we say that all have sinned?

To "sin" is to do wrong or to violate God's laws, and this meaning is certainly present in the Greek word translated "sinned" in Romans 3:23, which is *hamartano*. But one definition of hamartano is particularly interesting: simply, "to miss the mark."[3]

---

[3] Greek Lexicon: G264 (KJV). Retrieved January 12, 2015, from
http://www.blueletterbible.org/lang/lexicon/lexicon.cfm?Strongs=G264&t=KJV.

Sin itself is defined in English as "a vitiated state of human nature in which the self is estranged from God," and to sin is "to do something that is considered wrong according to religious or moral law."[4]

In short, then, to sin is to rebel against God and His authority. In the Garden of Eden, Adam and Eve chose to disobey God. As a consequence, each of their descendants is born into a condition of estrangement from God. Sadly, as we advance through life, sin tightens its grip on us and leads us steadily away from God and toward our doom.

> *"...By one man sin entered into the world, and death by sin; and so death passed upon all men, for that all have sinned" (Romans 5:12).*

The Call to Repentance

Despite the fact that all have sinned and offended Him, God's love and mercy are so powerful that He does not wish us any harm. His desire is that we recognize the error of our ways and come to Him in repentance.

> *"The Lord is not slack concerning his promise, as some men count slackness; but is longsuffering to us-ward, not willing that any should perish but that all should come to repentance" (II Peter 3:9).*

---

[4] "Sin." *Merriam-Webster.com.* Merriam-Webster, n.d. Web. 12 Jan. 2015. <http://www.merriam-webster.com/dictionary/sin>.

However, we must not interpret His mercy and grace as meaning that He really doesn't care about our sins. He does. In fact, the Scripture tells us that He **commands** all men everywhere to repent.

> *"And the times of this ignorance God winked at; but now commandeth all men every where to repent" (Acts 17:30).*

Repentance is absolutely essential to salvation. Any attempt to progress in your walk with God without a real repentance experience will result in much frustration, and, ultimately, in miserable failure. The Apostle Paul explains to us the Gospel, and tells us that it is the death, burial, resurrection, and appearing of the Lord.

> *"Moreover, brethren, I declare unto you the gospel which I preached unto you, which also ye have received, and wherein ye stand; by which also ye are saved, if ye keep in memory what I preached unto you, unless ye have believed in vain. For I delivered unto you first of all that which I also received, how that <u>Christ died</u> for our sins according to the scriptures; and that <u>he was buried</u>, and that <u>he rose again</u> the third day according to the scriptures: and that <u>he was seen</u> of Cephas, then of the twelve..." I Corinthians 15:1-5.*

Therefore, we experience the Gospel in our own lives when we repent (die to our sins), are baptized in Jesus' name (are buried with Him – see

Colossians 2:12), receive the gift of the Holy Ghost (are resurrected to walk with Him in newness of life – see Romans 6:4), and live a life of holiness and separation from sin, thus allowing the world to see Jesus in us (Hebrews 12:14). (See Acts 2:38). Notice that burial and resurrection would be pointless if not preceded by death. By the same token, water baptism and receiving the Holy Ghost serve no purpose unless we have first repented of our sins.

> *"Buried with him in baptism, wherein also ye are risen with him through the faith of the operation of God, who hath raised him from the dead" (Colossians 2:12).*
> *"Therefore we are buried with him by baptism into death: that like as Christ was raised up from the dead by the glory of the Father, even so we also should walk in newness of life" (Romans 6:4).*
> *"Follow peace with all men, and holiness, without which no man shall see the Lord" (Hebrews 12:14).*
> *"Then Peter said unto them, Repent, and be baptized every one of you in the name of Jesus Christ for the remission of sins, and ye shall receive the gift of the Holy Ghost...and with many other words did he testify and exhort, saying, Save yourselves from this untoward generation" (Acts 2:38, 40).*
> *"I tell you, Nay: but, except ye repent, ye shall all likewise perish" (Luke 13:3).*

The Meaning of "Repentance"

It is vitally important to understand the difference between "repentance" and "reformation." *Reformation* is defined as "the act or process of improving something or someone by removing or correcting faults, problems, etc."[5] – basically, it's our attempt to fix ourselves. While we may be able to achieve a certain degree of success in repressing our sinful desires and controlling our behavior, the change is only external. Inside, we still wrestle with our old human nature, and struggle to control our negative impulses. Perhaps the most important thing to note about mere reformation is that, while it may make us a better person, it will do nothing to help us be saved. It is entirely a personal enterprise.

Repentance, on the other hand, is a process that depends entirely on divine intervention for success. When you repent of your sins, you realize that you have failed to meet God's expectations and turn to Him for help in living the way He wants you to. Repentance involves a miracle from God! Success is not up to you – it is up to Him. Once you understand this, everything else makes sense.

The Greek word translated "repent" in scriptures like Acts 2:38 is *metanoeo*, which means "to change one's mind, i.e. to repent, or to change one's mind for better, heartily to amend with abhorrence of

---

[5] "Reformation." *Merriam-Webster.com*. Merriam-Webster, n.d. Web. 12 Jan. 2015. <http://www.merriam-webster.com/dictionary/reformation>.

one's past sins."[6] In English, "repent" is defined as follows: "*intransitive senses* 1: to turn from sin and dedicate oneself to the amendment of one's life 2 a: to feel regret or contrition b: to change one's mind; *transitive senses* 1: to cause to feel regret or contrition 2: to feel sorrow, regret, or contrition for."[7] We can further define "repentance" as 1) to turn around; a total change of direction; a 180° turn, 2) a change of attitude (especially toward God), 3) to abandon sin and turn to God, and 4) to recognize that you have offended God, and to feel sorrow for doing so; to make the decision to never again, by the grace of God, return to your past sins. Notice that the Bible emphasizes not only confessing but *forsaking* sin.

> *"He that covereth his sins shall not prosper: but whoso confesseth and forsaketh them shall have mercy" (Proverbs 28:13).*

You must understand that repentance will never work without faith in the operation of God. It is not the will of God for an alcoholic to take six months to "dry out", or for a tobacco addict to have to go through withdrawals in order to quit smoking. True repentance looks to God for deliverance, and He immediately and completely sets the person free of

---

[6] Greek Lexicon: G3340 (KJV). Retrieved from http://www.blueletterbible.org/lang/lexicon/lexicon.cfm?Strongs=G3340&t=KJV.

[7] "Repent." *Merriam-Webster.com*. Merriam-Webster, n.d. Web. 12 Jan. 2015. <http://www.merriam-webster.com/dictionary/repent>.

his or her negative habits through His miraculous power. It is essential that you believe this! God is able to deliver you instantly.

Repentance does not *suppress* a person's negative desires – it *kills* them. When we repent, we die to our sins. That is why we are no longer under their power. However, we cannot remain in that condition or sin will resurrect and dominate us again. As we will see in the next few lessons, we must proceed to bury the "old man" that we have put to death by being baptized in water in the name of Jesus Christ. Then He will raise us up to walk with Him in a new life. This is called receiving the baptism of the Holy Ghost. Once we have experienced this, we will be completely new creations, free from the power of sin that dominated our "old man".

> *"Therefore if any man be in Christ, he is a new creature: old things are passed away; behold, all things are become new" (II Corinthians 5:17).*

Total Separation from the World

Repentance is a radical experience, and should not be entered into rashly. When you repent you make promises to God that must be kept, even when the emotion of the moment is past. You must realize that repentance will demand a drastic change in your lifestyle. If you are not willing to commit to this, you have not truly repented.

A heart that is genuinely repentant will not desire any association with the sinful elements of the world. In fact, the Bible says that if you do love the world, the love of God is not in you!

> *"Love not the world, neither the things that are in the world. If any man love the world, the love of the Father is not in him. For all that is in the world, the lust of the flesh, and the lust of the eyes, and the pride of life, is not of the Father, but is of the world"* (I John 2:15-16).

Once you have repented, you should not desire to resemble the world in your appearance, your clothing and styles, your music, your hairstyles, your speech, your ambitions, or in any other way. Look at what the Bible has to say on the subject:

> *"And be not conformed to this world: but be ye transformed by the renewing of your mind, that ye may prove what is that good, and acceptable, and perfect, will of God"* (Romans 12:2).
>
> *"But every woman that prayeth or prophesieth with her head uncovered dishonoureth her head: for that is even all one as if she were shaven. For if the woman be not covered, let her also be shorn: but if it be a shame for a woman to be shorn or shaven, let her be covered... But if a woman have long hair, it is a glory to her: for her hair is given her for a covering"* (I Corinthians 11:5-6, 15).

> *"Every man praying or prophesying, having his head covered, dishonoureth his head. Doth not even nature itself teach you, that, if a man have long hair, it is a shame unto him?" (I Corinthians 11:4, 14).*
>
> *"Let no man despise thy youth; but be thou an example of the believers, in word, in conversation, in charity, in spirit, in faith, in purity" (I Timothy 4:12).*
>
> *"But seek ye first the kingdom of God, and his righteousness; and all these things shall be added unto you" (Matthew 6:33).*

Many people try to "straddle the fence" and see just how close they can get to the world and still be saved. The truly repentant heart, however, is guided by this question: What can I do to draw closer to God, and to be more acceptable in His sight?

> *"I beseech you therefore, brethren, by the mercies of God, that ye present your bodies a living sacrifice, holy, acceptable unto God, which is your reasonable service" (Romans 12:1).*

God looks at our lives to see if we are living in a way that reflects a true repentance experience. He expects us to produce "fruits meet for repentance." This means there will be a **measurable change** in our lives as a result of repenting of our sins.

> *"But when he saw many of the Pharisees and Sadducees come to his baptism, he said unto*

them, O generation of vipers, who hath warned you to flee from the wrath to come? Bring forth therefore fruits meet for repentance: and think not to say within yourselves, We have Abraham to our father: for I say unto you, that God is able of these stones to raise up children unto Abraham" (Matthew 3:7-9).

A Repented Heart Makes Restitution

When someone truly repents, he or she becomes responsible for righting any past wrongs that can be righted. The first responsibility, of course, is to correct wrongs committed against God. This is accomplished by confessing sin, abandoning it, and burying it in water baptism in Jesus' name. We can then be certain that we have settled our account with God.

"Repent ye therefore, and be converted, that your sins may be blotted out, when the times of refreshing shall come from the presence of the Lord." (Acts 3:19).

Next, we must make restitution to others. If we have stolen, we must make an effort to repay what we have taken. If we have harmed people in other ways, we must do whatever possible to make things right. This is not easy, but the rewards are eternal!

"And Zacchaeus stood, and said unto the Lord; Behold, Lord, the half of my goods I give to the poor; and if I have taken any thing from any

> *man by false accusation, I restore him fourfold" (Luke 19:8).*
>
> *"If the wicked restore the pledge, give again that he had robbed, walk in the statutes of life, without committing iniquity; he shall surely live, he shall not die. None of his sins that he hath committed shall be mentioned unto him: he hath done that which is lawful and right; he shall surely live" (Ezekiel 33:15-16).*

Finally, we must make restitution to ourselves. By living in sin in the past and catering to the desires of our flesh, we placed ourselves on a pathway that would lead us to eternal damnation in the flames of hell. Often, we engaged in practices and habits that were harmful to our bodies. When we repent, we change our course and set a new destination: Heaven. We also make changes in our lifestyle that result in better care of our bodies, because they now become, upon receiving the gift of the Holy Ghost, the temple of the Holy Spirit of God.

> *"Know ye not that ye are the temple of God, and that the Spirit of God dwelleth in you? If any man defile the temple of God, him shall God destroy; for the temple of God is holy, which temple ye are" (I Corinthians 3:16-17).*

We will talk more about receiving the Holy ghost in a future chapter. Meanwhile, consider this: while the consequences of a failure to repent are severe in that the Bible says that the soul that sins shall die, the promises of God for those who repent are glorious!

> *"The soul that sinneth, it shall die..." (Ezekiel 18:20a).*
> *"I tell you, Nay: but, except ye repent, ye shall all likewise perish" (Luke 13:3)*
> *"If my people, which are called by my name, shall humble themselves, and pray, and seek my face, and turn from their wicked ways; then will I hear from heaven, and will forgive their sin, and will heal their land" (II Chronicles 7:14).*
> *"Say unto them, As I live, saith the Lord God, I have no pleasure in the death of the wicked; but that the wicked turn from his way and live: turn ye, turn ye from your evil ways; for why will ye die, O house of Israel?...But if the wicked turn from his wickedness, and do that which is lawful and right, he shall live thereby" (Ezekiel 33:11, 19).*

If you have not yet repented, why don't you pray right now and let God begin the miracle of deliverance from sin in your life?

Chapter 4: Water Baptism

Water baptism is no doubt the most important ceremony in which you will ever participate. It is more than just a religious rite or tradition; in baptism, your sins are forgiven, and your "old man" is buried with Jesus Christ, just as we studied in the lesson on repentance.

> *"Then Peter said unto them, Repent, and be baptized every one of you in the name of Jesus Christ for the remission of sins, and ye shall receive the gift of the Holy Ghost" (Acts 2:38)*
> *"Buried with him in baptism, wherein also ye are risen with him through the faith of the operation of God, who hath raised him from the dead" (Colossians 2:12).*

In addition, water baptism is a part of the new birth of which Jesus spoke in John 3:5.

> *"Jesus answered, Verily, verily, I say unto thee, Except a man be born of water and of the Spirit, he cannot enter into the kingdom of God."*

Many churches deny that water baptism is a part of the new birth, claiming instead that when Jesus spoke of being "born of water", He was referring to the amniotic fluid of the womb. Let's take a good look at this. Jesus never wasted words; in fact, He cautioned against the use of idle words

(Matthew 12:36). Since every human being that has ever been born into this world was born of the amniotic fluid, why would Jesus list this as a requirement to enter the kingdom of God? If you take a good look at the context of this passage, you will find that Jesus was not speaking of natural childbirth, as He specifically stated that "ye must be born again" (John 3:3, 7). He was not telling Nicodemus what he had *already done*; He was telling him what he *needed to do*. Therefore, He could not have been speaking of the amniotic fluid. We will prove conclusively, as the lesson goes on, that He was speaking of water baptism.

> *"There was a man of the Pharisees, named Nicodemus, a ruler of the Jews: the same came to Jesus by night, and said unto him, Rabbi, we know that thou art a teacher come from God: for no man can do these miracles that thou doest, except God be with him. Jesus answered and said unto him, Verily, verily, I say unto thee, Except a man be born again, he cannot see the kingdom of God. Nicodemus saith unto him, How can a man be born when he is old? can he enter the second time into his mother's womb, and be born? Jesus answered, Verily, verily, I say unto thee, Except a man be born of water and of the Spirit, he cannot enter into the kingdom of God. That which is born of the flesh is flesh; and that which is born of the Spirit is spirit. Marvel not that I said unto thee, Ye must be born again" (John 3:1-7)*

Water baptism is also an identification with Jesus Christ. His name is pronounced over us when we are baptized.

> *"And now why tarriest thou? arise, and be baptized, and wash away thy sins, calling on the name of the Lord" (Acts 22:16).*

The Necessity of Water Baptism

The Scripture is clear regarding the fact that you absolutely must be "born of water" in order to enter the kingdom of God. Jesus stated this in the passage we have just read from the third chapter of John. He also said in Mark 16:16 that he that believes and is baptized shall be saved.

> *"He that believeth and is baptized shall be saved; but he that believeth not shall be damned" (Mark 16:16).*

The Apostle Peter agreed completely with Jesus in his writings. This is what he had to say about baptism:

> *"The like figure whereunto even baptism doth also now save us (not the putting away of the filth of the flesh, but the answer of a good conscience toward God,) by the resurrection of Jesus Christ" (I Peter 3:21).*

Lest we create the impression that water baptism alone saves us, remember that Jesus said we must be born of water *and* of the Spirit (one birth, two elements). Ephesians 4:5 says there is only one baptism, so we must conclude that the baptism that saves us is a baptism consisting of two elements: the physical (water baptism) and the spiritual (baptism in the Holy Ghost). This agrees perfectly with the message Peter preached on the day of Pentecost, in Acts 2:38. We will study more about the spiritual element of baptism in the next chapter.

> *"One Lord, one faith, one baptism" (Ephesians 4:5).*
> *"Then Peter said unto them, Repent, and be baptized every one of you in the name of Jesus Christ for the remission of sins, and ye shall receive the gift of the Holy Ghost" (Acts 2:38).*

The Purpose of Water Baptism

Let's look at the purpose of water baptism. While baptism does have other purposes such as identification with Jesus Christ, it is safe to say that the primary purpose of water baptism is for the forgiveness of sins. The word rendered *"remission"* in the King James translation of Acts 2:38 comes from the word *aphesis* in the original Greek. This word not only means "remission" (sending away), but also *"forgiveness."*[8] We must be careful of a very common doctrine that teaches that forgiveness

---

[8] Greek Lexicon: G859 (KJV). Retrieved from http://www.blueletterbible.org/lang/lexicon/lexicon.cfm?Strongs=G859&t=KJV.

of sins is received at repentance (for a sinner who has not yet been baptized in water). This invalidates the core reason for baptism. If we study the Scriptures carefully, we will see that in repentance we **ask** God to forgive us, and in water baptism we **receive** His forgiveness, because we have obeyed His Word by faith. Biblically, forgiveness of sins is only achieved through a combination of faith, repentance, and water baptism in Jesus' name.

> *"Then Peter said unto them, Repent, and be baptized every one of you in the name of Jesus Christ for the remission of sins, and ye shall receive the gift of the Holy Ghost" (Acts 2:38).*

For a more thorough discussion of the term aphesis and its meaning of remission/forgiveness, please see Appendix A.

Baptism washes away our sins – not the water that is applied to our bodies, but what it symbolizes: the blood of Jesus that is applied to our hearts. It is the answer to repentance; at repentance, we die to sin; in baptism, we bury the old man with his sins.

> *"And now why tarriest thou? arise, and be baptized, and wash away thy sins, calling on the name of the Lord" (Acts 22:16).*
>
> *"In whom also ye are circumcised with the circumcision made without hands, in putting off the body of the sins of the flesh by the circumcision of Christ: buried with him in baptism, wherein also ye are risen with him through the faith of the operation of God, who*

hath raised him from the dead" (Colossians 2:11-12).

The Biblical Method of Baptism

Although much controversy surrounds the issue of which is the proper mode of baptism, it is really quite a simple subject. If we look at what was said in the original text, it leaves no doubt whatsoever as to which method is correct. The ***only*** method of baptism presented in the Bible is by immersion. In fact, the very word "baptism" comes from the Greek word *baptizo*, which literally means to "dip" or to "submerge."[9] Therefore, when Jesus and His disciples commanded baptism, they were literally commanding to dip or to submerge. If you had been present on the Day of Pentecost in Acts chapter 2, you would have heard Peter say, "Repent, and every one of you be dipped in the name of Jesus Christ, in order that your sins may be forgiven...." This is only logical, since (as we have already seen) both Romans 6:4 and Colossians 2:12 tell us that we are buried with Him by baptism. No one buries their dead by simply sprinkling a handful of dirt on them!

Let's look at the following Scriptural accounts of baptism to see if they are consistent with baptism

---

[9] Greek Lexicon: G907 (KJV). Retrieved from http://www.blueletterbible.org/lang/lexicon/lexicon.cfm?Strongs=G907&t=KJV.

by immersion. Remember, Ephesians 4:5 says there is only one baptism; therefore, if the John the Baptist and the preachers of the early church did it this way in these accounts, we must conclude they did it this way all the time.

1. After He was baptized, Jesus "went up straightway out of the water;" this clearly implies that Jesus entered the water to be baptized, which would have been pointless had He not been baptized by immersion.
   "And Jesus, when he was baptized, went up straightway out of the water: and, lo, the heavens were opened unto him, and he saw the Spirit of God descending like a dove, and lighting upon him" (Matthew 3:16).
2. John the Baptist was baptizing in a certain place because "there was much water there;" this would have been unnecessary had he been baptizing by sprinkling.
   "And John also was baptizing in Aenon near to Salim, because there was much water there: and they came, and were baptized" (John 3:23).
3. The Ethiopian eunuch was baptized in a place where there was water; doubtless, he had a bottle of water with him, as he was travelling through the desert, but the Scripture says he and Philip "went down both into the water".
   "And as they went on their way, they came unto a certain water: and the eunuch said,

See, here is water; what doth hinder me to be baptized? And Philip said, If thou believest with all thine heart, thou mayest. And he answered and said, I believe that Jesus Christ is the Son of God. And he commanded the chariot to stand still: and they went down both into the water, both Philip and the eunuch; and he baptized him" (Acts 8:36-38).

4. Verse 39 says, "when they were come up out of the water...." Therefore, it is obvious that they went all the way down into the water.

    "And when they were come up out of the water, the Spirit of the Lord caught away Philip, that the eunuch saw him no more: and he went on his way rejoicing" (Acts 8:39).

Who May Be Baptized?

While it is certainly the will of God that everyone be baptized, we must also be aware that the Word of God has established certain prerequisites that must be met in order to qualify for baptism. First of all, as we already studied in the chapter on faith, a person must believe.

"He that believeth and is baptized shall be saved; but he that believeth not shall be damned" (Mark 16:16).
"And Philip said, If thou believest with all thine heart, thou mayest. And he answered and said,

*I believe that Jesus Christ is the Son of God"
(Acts 8:37).*

Next, as we also studied in the chapter on repentance, a person must repent of his or her sins.

"But when he saw many of the Pharisees and Sadducees come to his baptism, he said unto them, O generation of vipers, who hath warned you to flee from the wrath to come? Bring forth therefore fruits meet for repentance" (Matthew 3:7-8).
"Then Peter said unto them, Repent, and be baptized every one of you in the name of Jesus Christ for the remission of sins, and ye shall receive the gift of the Holy Ghost" (Acts 2:38).

Because believing and repenting of one's sins are prerequisites to baptism, it is not Biblically appropriate to baptize infants nor children too young to understand the meaning of baptism, and the need thereof. In fact, there is no mention of infant baptism before the second century A.D.,[10] meaning infant baptism is a practice that was instituted by the Roman Catholic Church long after Jesus ascended and the apostles died, and was therefore unknown to the early church.

Observe, too, that because baptism means to dip or submerge (which is not likely to happen in "infant baptism"), true infant baptism is really not even a viable consideration.

---

[10] Martin, L. (1987, October 1). The History of Infant Baptism. *Guardian of Truth*, XXXI:19, 584-586.

It's also worth mentioning that not everyone is qualified to be immediately baptized. When unrepentant people came to him for baptism, John the Baptist would send them away with a stern warning that they should first produce fruit or evidence of repentance. Today is no exception; if a person continues to live in sin, he or she has not demonstrated true repentance. That is why it is improper for people living together without the benefit of marriage to be baptized until they have either married or separated. For a deeper discussion of this subject, see Appendix B.

What Is the Proper Baptismal Formula?

We must pay close attention to the Biblical formula for baptism, for, as we will see shortly, it is crucial to obtaining the forgiveness of our sins. The fact that something is widely used does not necessarily mean it is correct. When it comes to matters as serious as how to be baptized, we must rely on the Bible as our sole authority, and not trust to tradition or post-apostolic church leaders.

In Matthew 28:19, Jesus commanded His apostles to baptize all nations "in the name of the Father, and of the Son, and of the Holy Ghost."

> *"Go ye therefore, and teach all nations, baptizing them in the name of the Father, and of the Son, and of the Holy Ghost" (Matthew 28:19).*

Unfortunately, many people today only repeat this commandment without studying it carefully to make sure they really understand it, and therefore actually fail to obey the commandment.

In the first place, Jesus commanded to baptize *in the name* (singular, only one name) of the Father, and of the Son, and of the Holy Ghost, and did not command that His words be *repeated,* which is what most denominations do today. "Father," "Son," and "Holy Ghost" are not names; they are *titles*. If someone baptizes using these titles, they have not baptized in any name!

To illustrate this point, let's take a look at this sentence's grammatical structure. "Of the Father," "of the Son," and "of the Holy Ghost" are all prepositional phrases that refer back to one singular name ("in the name"). As we will see, the name of the Father, and of the Son, and of the Holy Ghost is Jesus.

According to Isaiah 9:6, John 5:43, John 10:30, and John 14:6-10, the Father dwelt in and was one with the body of Jesus, thus making Jesus the Father manifested (made visible) in the flesh (II Corinthians 5:19; I Timothy 3:16); therefore, the name of the Father is clearly Jesus.

> *"For unto us a child is born, unto us a son is given: and the government shall be upon his shoulder: and his name shall be called Wonderful, Counsellor, The mighty God, the everlasting Father, The Prince of Peace"* *(Isaiah 9:6).*

"I am come in my Father's name, and ye receive me not: if another shall come in his own name, him ye will receive" (John 5:43).

"I and my Father are one" (John 10:30).

"Jesus saith unto him, I am the way, the truth, and the life: no man cometh unto the Father, but by me. If ye had known me, ye should have known my Father also: and from henceforth ye know him, and have seen him. Philip saith unto him, Lord, shew us the Father, and it sufficeth us. Jesus saith unto him, have I been so long time with you, and yet hast thou not known me, Philip? he that hath seen me hath seen the Father; and how sayest thou then, Shew us the Father? Believest thou not that I am in the Father, and the Father in me? the words that I speak unto you I speak not of myself: but the Father that dwelleth in me, he doeth the works" (John 14:6-10).

"To wit, that God was in Christ, reconciling the world unto himself, not imputing their trespasses unto them; and hath committed unto us the word of reconciliation" (II Corinthians 5:19).

"And without controversy great is the mystery of godliness: God was manifest in the flesh, justified in the Spirit, seen of angels, preached unto the Gentiles, believed on in the world, received up into glory" (I Timothy 3:16).

According to Matthew 1:21, Jesus, as the human body in which the Father manifested Himself, was also the Son, born of a woman;

therefore, beyond a shadow of a doubt, the name of the Son is Jesus (Mark 1:1).

> *"And she shall bring forth a son, and thou shalt call his name JESUS: for he shall save his people from their sins" (Matthew 1:21).*
> *"The beginning of the gospel of Jesus Christ, the Son of God" (Mark 1:1).*

What is the name of the Holy Ghost? We can find out beyond a shadow of a doubt by studying this sequence of Bible verses:

1. Jesus is Lord (Philippians 2:10-11)
2. There is only one Lord (Ephesians 4:5)
3. The Lord (Jesus) is the Spirit (II Corinthians 3:17)
4. There is only one Spirit (Ephesians 4:4); therefore, the name of the Holy Ghost (Holy Spirit) is clearly Jesus.

> *"That at the name of Jesus every knee should bow, of things in heaven, and things in earth, and things under the earth; and that every tongue should confess that <u>Jesus Christ is Lord</u>, to the glory of God the Father" (Philippians 2:10-11).*
> *"<u>One Lord</u>, one faith, one baptism" (Ephesians 4:5).*
> *"Now <u>the Lord is that Spirit</u>: and where the Spirit of the Lord is, there is liberty" (II Corinthians 3:17).*

"There is one body, and <u>one Spirit</u>, even as ye are called in one hope of your calling" (Ephesians 4:4).

To see if we have correctly interpreted Jesus' commandment to baptize "in the name of the Father, and of the Son, and of the Holy Ghost," let's see how the apostles obeyed it. If we find they consistently baptized in the name of Jesus Christ, then we know we are on the right track.

Interestingly enough, there are several examples in the Bible where the apostles and early church preachers obeyed Jesus' commandment to baptize, but there is not a **single instance** where they baptized using the words "in the name of the Father, and of the Son, and of the Holy Ghost;" ***this never happened.*** Without exception, when the apostles baptized, they baptized in the "name of the Lord," in the "name of the Lord Jesus," or in the "name of Jesus Christ." Look at this list:

1. In the name of Jesus Christ.
    "Then Peter said unto them, Repent, and be baptized every one of you in the name of Jesus Christ for the remission of sins, and ye shall receive the gift of the Holy Ghost" (Acts 2:38).
2. In the name of the Lord Jesus.
    "(For as yet he was fallen upon none of them: only they were baptized in the name of the Lord Jesus)" (Acts 8:16).
3. In the name of the Lord.

> *"And he commanded them to be baptized in the name of the Lord. Then prayed they him to tarry certain days" (Acts 10:48).*

4. In the name of the Lord Jesus.
   > *"When they heard this, they were baptized in the name of the Lord Jesus" (Acts 19:5).*
5. Calling on the name of the Lord.
   > *"And now why tarriest thou? arise, and be baptized, and wash away thy sins, calling on the name of the Lord" (Acts 22:16).*

Baptism using the titles "Father, Son, and Holy Ghost" was never practiced by the apostles nor by the New Testament church; in fact, it appears to have been adopted near (at the earliest) the end of the first century or sometime in the second century, and even critics of baptism in Jesus' name concede that the Trinitarian formula "can be considered an expansion of an earlier, purely christological one."[11] Of course, here "christological" refers simply to the baptismal formula using the name of Jesus.

Why is it so urgent that we be baptized in the name of Jesus? There are several reasons:

1. No other name has power to save.
   > *"Neither is there salvation in any other: for there is none other name under heaven given among men, whereby we must be saved" (Acts 4:12).*
2. A person who is baptized using the titles "Father, Son, and Holy Ghost" has not been

---

[11] Hultrgren, A. (1994). Baptism in the New Testament: Origins, Formulas, and Metaphors. *Word & World, 14*(1), 6-11.

baptized in any name, and, therefore, does not receive salvation, according to Acts 4:12.
3. The Bible says remission of sins comes "through his name;" therefore, unless you are baptized in His name, you do not receive the forgiveness of your sins.

"To him give all the prophets witness, that through his name whosoever believeth in him shall receive remission of sins" (Acts 10:43).

Do I Need to be Rebaptized?

Perhaps this chapter has raised some questions in your mind. You may be wondering, "Do I need to be rebaptized?" If you were not baptized in the name of Jesus, it is not a matter of "rebaptism," for no other baptism is biblically valid (Ephesians 4:5). According to the Bible, it is both proper and necessary for someone who has been baptized with another baptism to be baptized again in the name of Jesus.

"And it came to pass, that, while Apollos was at Corinth, Paul having passed through the upper coasts came to Ephesus: and finding certain disciples, he said unto them, Have ye received the Holy Ghost since ye believed? And they said unto him, We have not so much as heard whether there be any Holy Ghost. And he said unto them, Unto what then were ye baptized? And they said, Unto John's baptism.

Then said Paul, John verily baptized with the baptism of repentance, saying unto the people, that they should believe on him which should come after him, that is, on Christ Jesus. When they heard this, they were baptized in the name of the Lord Jesus. And when Paul had laid his hands upon them, the Holy Ghost came on them; and they spake with tongues, and prophesied" (Acts 19:1-6).

If you have yet to be baptized in the name of Jesus Christ, please consider this question straight from the Word of God:

"And now why tarriest thou? arise, and be baptized, and wash away thy sins, calling on the name of the Lord" (Acts 22:16).

Chapter 5: The Baptism of the Holy Ghost

The Holy Ghost is known in the Bible by various titles, such as "the Holy Spirit," "the Spirit of God," "the Spirit," "the Spirit of the Lord," "the Spirit of Christ," "the Spirit of Jesus," "the Spirit of Jesus Christ," "the Spirit of Truth" and "the Comforter." However, all of these titles refer to the same divine Being.

Perhaps the best way to begin a discussion about the Holy Ghost is to simply say that He is God.

> *"God is a Spirit: and they that worship him must worship him in spirit and in truth" (John 4:24).*
>
> *"Now the Lord is that Spirit: and where the Spirit of the Lord is, there is liberty" (II Corinthians 3:17).*

Specifically, the Holy Ghost is none other than the spirit of the Lord Jesus Christ.

> *"But ye are not in the flesh, but in the Spirit, if so be that the Spirit of God dwell in you. Now if any man have not the Spirit of Christ, he is none of his" (Romans 8:9).*

> *"For I know that this shall turn to my salvation through your prayer, and the supply of the Spirit of Jesus Christ" (Philippians 1:19).*

Lest you become confused by the Bible's use of many different titles for the Holy Ghost, remember that the Scriptures clearly establish the fact that there is only one divine Spirit.

> *"There is one body, and one Spirit, even as ye are called in one hope of your calling" (Ephesians 4:4).*

When the Bible refers to God as the Holy Ghost, it is normally referring specifically to God in operation. The one true God has revealed Himself in different ways to suit His purpose at different times: as the Father in creation, as the Son in redemption, and, today, as the Holy Ghost in operation in His church. Each one of His manifestations has a specific function.

What is the Gift of the Holy Ghost?

The simplest way to define the gift of the Holy Ghost is to say that when we receive the gift of the Holy Ghost, the Spirit of Jesus literally comes to live inside our bodies.

"To whom God would make known what is the riches of the glory of this mystery among the Gentiles; which is Christ in you, the hope of glory" (Colossians 1:27).

"Even the Spirit of truth; whom the world cannot receive, because it seeth him not, neither knoweth him: but ye know him; for he dwelleth with you, and shall be in you" (John 14:17).

No wonder Jesus said you would receive power after you receive the Holy Ghost! The great Creator of the universe, the Almighty God, lives inside of you!

The Purpose of the Gift of the Holy Ghost

There are many reasons why it is essential that we receive the gift of the Holy Ghost. Here are a few of them:

1. The Holy Ghost is the "visa" that grants us entry into the kingdom of God. A visa is a stamp (seal) in a passport that grants entry into a country (providing all other immigration requirements are met).
  "And grieve not the holy Spirit of God, whereby ye are sealed unto the day of redemption" (Ephesians 4:30).

"Jesus answered, Verily, verily, I say unto thee, Except a man be born of water and of the Spirit, he cannot enter into the kingdom of God" (John 3:5).

2. The gift of the Holy Ghost causes us to belong to God; without it, we cannot be saved.

    "But ye are not in the flesh, but in the Spirit, if so be that the Spirit of God dwell in you. Now if any man have not the Spirit of Christ, he is none of his" (Romans 8:9).

3. The gift of the Holy Ghost sets us free from sin.

    "Now the Lord is that Spirit: and where the Spirit of the Lord is, there is liberty" (II Corinthians 3:17).

4. The gift of the Holy Ghost teaches us the truth.

    "Howbeit when he, the Spirit of truth, is come, he will guide you into all truth: for he shall not speak of himself; but whatsoever he shall hear, that shall he speak: and he will shew you things to come" (John 16:13).

5. The gift of the Holy Ghost gives us comfort, joy, righteousness, and peace.

    "But the Comforter, which is the Holy Ghost, whom the Father will send in my name, he shall teach you all things, and bring all things to your remembrance,

whatsoever I have said unto you" (John 14:26).

"For the kingdom of God is not meat and drink; but righteousness, and peace, and joy in the Holy Ghost" (Romans 14:17).

6. The gift of the Holy Ghost fills us with the love of God.

    "And hope maketh not ashamed; because the love of God is shed abroad in our hearts by the Holy Ghost which is given unto us" (Romans 5:5).

7. The gift of the Holy Ghost sanctifies us, in whom no good thing dwells naturally, by placing His holy nature within us.

    "For I know that in me (that is, in my flesh,) dwelleth no good thing: for to will is present with me; but how to perform that which is good I find not" (Romans 7:18).

    "And such were some of you: but ye are washed, but ye are sanctified, but ye are justified in the name of the Lord Jesus, and by the Spirit of our God" (I Corinthians 6:11).

8. The gift of the Holy Ghost gives us power to be witnesses.

    "But ye shall receive power, after that the Holy Ghost is come upon you: and ye shall be witnesses unto me both in Jerusalem, and

in all Judaea, and in Samaria, and unto the uttermost part of the earth" (Acts 1:8).*

9. The gift of the Holy Ghost will resurrect us at the coming of the Lord.

    "But if the Spirit of him that raised up Jesus from the dead dwell in you, he that raised up Christ from the dead shall also quicken your mortal bodies by his Spirit that dwelleth in you" (Romans 8:11).

Receiving the Gift of the Holy Ghost

Contrary to what many churches teach today, the gift of the Holy Ghost is not something that is received automatically and without external evidence when a person is water baptized. We can look to the Biblical account of the conversion of the Samaritans to prove this.

"Now when the apostles which were at Jerusalem heard that Samaria had received the word of God, they sent unto them Peter and John: Who, when they were come down, prayed for them, that they might receive the Holy Ghost: (For as yet he was fallen upon none of them: only they were baptized in the name of the Lord Jesus.) Then laid they their hands on them, and they received the Holy Ghost" (Acts 8:14-17).

Notice that the Samaritans had **already** been baptized in water in the name of the Lord Jesus, but still had not received the gift of the Holy Ghost.

Another good example is Cornelius, along with his household. In their case, they received the gift of the Holy Ghost **before** they were water baptized:

> *"While Peter yet spake these words, the Holy Ghost fell on all them which heard the word" (Acts 10:44).*
> *"Can any man forbid water, that these should not be baptized, which have received the Holy Ghost as well as we?" (Acts 10:47).*

How, then, does one receive the gift of the Holy Ghost? There are several things we must understand. First of all, the Holy Ghost is received by faith.

> *"In the last day, that great day of the feast, Jesus stood and cried, saying, If any man thirst, let him come unto me, and drink. He that believeth on me, as the scripture hath said, out of his belly shall flow rivers of living water. (But this spake he of the Spirit, which they that believe on him should receive...)" (John 7:37-39).*

Second, the Holy Ghost is received through obedience to God.

> *"And we are his witnesses of these things; and so is also the Holy Ghost, whom God hath given to them that obey him" (Acts 5:32).*
>
> *"Then Peter said unto them, Repent, and be baptized every one of you in the name of Jesus Christ for the remission of sins, and ye shall receive the gift of the Holy Ghost" (Acts 2:38).*

The Sign of Receiving the Gift of the Holy Ghost

Since receiving the Holy Ghost is so essential to our salvation, God has chosen to give us a miraculous and unmistakable sign when He fills someone with His Spirit. This way, there will be no doubt that that person has received the gift of the Holy Ghost.

The sign God has chosen is known in the Bible as "speaking with other tongues," or "speaking in tongues." This phenomenon occurs when God, to signal that He is now indwelling a person, uses that individual's tongue to speak in a language he or she does not understand while praying and worshiping.

Why did God choose something as dramatic and supernatural as speaking in tongues? The Bible gives us a clear answer: the tongue is the one thing that man has been unable to tame by his own strength. How many times have we regretted things our tongue has uttered, that in some cases have caused irreparable harm! If you want to know just how untamable the tongue is, try to learn a foreign language with the skill and accent of a native speaker. Your tongue will rebel at the strange sounds a new language requires. So what better way for God to show He is now in control of our body than for Him to take our tongue and do what we cannot do: instantly cause it to speak fluently in a language we have never studied?

Consider what the Apostle James had to say about the tongue:

> *"For in many things we offend all. If any man offend not in word, the same is a perfect man, and able also to bridle the whole body. Behold, we put bits in the horses' mouths, that they may obey us; and we turn about their whole body. Behold also the ships, which though they be so great, and are driven of fierce winds, yet are they turned about with a very small helm, whithersoever the governor listeth. Even so the tongue is a little member, and boasteth great things. Behold, how great a matter a little fire kindleth! And the tongue is a fire, a world of iniquity: so is the tongue among our members, that it defileth the whole body, and setteth on fire the course of nature; and it is set on fire of*

hell. For every kind of beasts, and of birds, and of serpents, and of things in the sea, is tamed, and hath been tamed of mankind: But the tongue can no man tame; it is an unruly evil, full of deadly poison" (James 3:2-8).

"We all make many mistakes, but those who control their tongues can also control themselves in every other way" (James 3:2, New Living Translation).

Let's do a Biblical case study to determine whether speaking in tongues was the standard in the early New Testament church.

1. On the Day of Pentecost, when the gift of the Holy Ghost was poured out for the first time on the church, all who received the Holy Ghost spoke in tongues.

    "And they were all filled with the Holy Ghost, and began to speak with other tongues, as the Spirit gave them utterance" (Acts 2:4).

2. In Acts chapter 8 (verses 5-25), while tongues are not specifically mentioned, it is obvious that something phenomenal and highly unusual happened when the apostles prayed for the people to receive the Holy Ghost. Were this not the case, Simon the Magician would never have attempted to

purchase this awesome power. No need to purchase something that produces no visible or audible results! Since the other accounts of people in the Bible receiving the Holy Ghost clearly state that they spoke with tongues, there is no reason whatsoever to believe the Samaritans had a different experience. Remember, God is no respecter of persons, meaning He treats everyone the same, and two or three witnesses (scriptures, in this case) are sufficient to establish a matter as truth.

"Then Peter opened his mouth, and said, Of a truth I perceive that God is no respecter of persons" (Acts 10:34).

"...In the mouth of two or three witnesses shall every word be established" (II Corinthians 13:1).

3. Cornelius and his household spoke in tongues when they received the Holy Ghost.

"While Peter yet spake these words, the Holy Ghost fell on all them which heard the word. And they of the circumcision which believed were astonished, as many as came with Peter, because that on the Gentiles also was poured out the gift of the Holy Ghost. For they heard them speak with tongues, and magnify God..." (Acts 10:44-46a).

4. The Ephesian disciples spoke in tongues when they received the gift of the Holy Ghost.

   "And when Paul had laid his hands upon them, the Holy Ghost came on them; and they spake with tongues, and prophesied" (Acts 19:6).

5. Did the Apostles speak in tongues?

   "And when they were come in, they went up into an upper room, where abode both Peter, and James, and John, and Andrew, Philip, and Thomas, Bartholomew, and Matthew, James the son of Alphaeus, and Simon Zelotes, and Judas the brother of James" (Acts 1:13).

   "And they were all filled with the Holy Ghost, and began to speak with other tongues, as the Spirit gave them utterance" (Acts 2:4).

6. Did the Apostle Paul speak in tongues?

   "I thank my God, I speak with tongues more than ye all" (I Corinthians 14:18).

7. Since God is no respecter of persons, you, too, will speak in tongues when you receive the Holy Ghost!

   "Then Peter opened his mouth, and said, Of a truth I perceive that God is no respecter of persons" (Acts 10:34).

8. The promise is for you!

    "For the promise is unto you, and to your children, and to all that are afar off, even as many as the Lord our God shall call" (Acts 2:39).

    "If ye then, being evil, know how to give good gifts unto your children: how much more shall your heavenly Father give the Holy Spirit to them that ask him?" (Luke 11:13).

Conclusion

A building is only as strong as its foundation. As believers, it is extremely important that our faith be built upon the firm foundation of the Word of God.

There can be no doubt the Apostle Paul was inspired when he wrote that "the time will come when they will not endure sound doctrine; but after their own lusts shall they heap to themselves teachers, having itching ears" (II Timothy 4:3). If ever there as a need for men and women to get into the Word of God, it's now...and it is extremely critical that Apostolic Pentecostal believers fully understand the core, distinctive doctrines that set us apart from the rest of the religious world.

The doctrines we have covered in this book are basic and fundamental. Our treatment of these doctrines has been general and introductory in nature. It is my hope that your appetite has been whetted, and that you will search the Scriptures for an even better understanding.

These doctrines were selected because they are essential to salvation, and because Apostolics hold a very different perspective on them than do most other religious groups. In a future book we will take a look at other critical Apostolic doctrines, such as the operation of spiritual gifts and the need for holiness and separation unto the Lord.

Appendix A

Remission or Forgiveness?
Examining a False Conundrum in Apostolic Theology in the Light of Proper Hermeneutics and Biblical Context

Kelly Nix, DBA
Institute for Conservative Apostolic Theology
Presented at the ICAT Seminar on the New Birth
San Antonio, Texas
November 2, 2013

Remission or Forgiveness? Examining a False Conundrum in Apostolic Theology in the Light of Proper Hermeneutics and Biblical Context

For as long as the author of this paper can remember, the subject of remission and forgiveness has been divisive in North American Apostolic circles. The disagreement stems from the wording of a key scripture in Apostolic theology:

"Then Peter said unto them, Repent, and be baptized every one of you in the name of Jesus Christ for the remission of sins, and ye shall receive the gift of the Holy Ghost" (Acts 2:38, KJV).

More than Semantics

The use of the word "remission" in Acts 2:38 causes many Apostolic scholars to conclude that what happens at water baptism in Jesus' Name is something other than forgiveness of sins. This can largely be attributed to the etymology of the English word remit, which comes from the Latin *remittere*, meaning "to send back" ("Remit," 2013).

Based on this definition, some Apostolic scholars and theologians conclude that what Peter referred to in Acts 2:38 is a specific act of "sending away" sins, but this does not necessarily equate to the act of *forgiving* sins. The word "forgive" is defined as "to give up resentment of or claim to requital for," "to grant relief from payment of," and "to cease to feel resentment against" ("Forgive," 2013). These scholars believe, then, that forgiveness (when God ceases to feel resentment at the sinner over his sins" and remission (when God sends away the sinner's sins) are separate operations, the latter subsequent to the former; in other words, they contend that sins are *forgiven* at repentance and are *remitted* (sent or washed away) at baptism. A doctrinal publication from a well-known Apostolic organization asserts that "the only way to forgiveness of sin is through genuine, heartfelt repentance" (R. M. Davis (Ed.), 1985) – a statement that, while technically accurate, is woefully incomplete because it omits any direct reference to the role of water baptism in the forgiveness of sins. The same publication subsequently declares that "repentance brings a man under the manifold richness of the grace of God. Sins are then forgiven....," and "it is no wonder that Pentecostal altars ring out with the praise of rejoicing – the load and guilt of sin has lifted! The joy of forgiveness of sins can be fully understood only by partaking of this blessing in heartfelt repentance." While this unspeakable joy is indeed the emotion that results from having one's sins forgiven, repentance is not where the Bible indicates this operation takes place.

It is the contention of this author that the distinction between the operations of forgiveness and remission is not legitimate. One major derogatory mark against the argument of distinct operations of forgiveness and remission of sins is that it arises entirely from the English translation of the Scriptures, without due regard to treatment of the subject in the original languages of the Bible. Also, it is the belief of this author that much of the resistance within the Apostolic movement to unequivocally declaring that forgiveness of sins occurs at water baptism in the Name of Jesus Christ is derived from early 20th-century influences of the large Trinitarian Pentecostal movements, such as the Assemblies of God and the Church of God in Christ, among which many Oneness Apostolic pioneers had their roots. These movements deny to this day that water baptism is essential to the forgiveness of sins, describing it rather as an act subsequent to salvation ("Assemblies of God," 2010; "What we believe," 2013).

Appealing to the Original

What, then, is the position of the original languages on the remission/forgiveness conundrum? A critical consideration is the fact that the Greek does not use distinct words for "forgiveness" and "remission;" rather, it was the decision of the translators as to which word they used in which context in the English Bible. For example, the

Greek word translated "remission" in Acts 2:38 is *aphesis*, meaning literally "release from bondage or imprisonment," or "forgiveness or pardon, of sins (letting them go as if they had never been committed);" "remission of the penalty" ("Aphesis," 2013). However, in Ephesians 1:7, the same word *aphesis* is translated "forgiveness": "In whom we have redemption through his blood, the forgiveness of sins, according to the riches of his grace...." While the English appears to create a distinction, there is no difference in word usage in the original language; both use "aphesis."

This proves to be the case throughout the New Testament. There are 17 occurrences of *aphesis* in the New Testament; in the King James Version, in nine of these the word is translated "remission;" in seven, it is translated "forgiveness;" in one it is translated "deliverance;" and in one it is rendered "liberty" ("Aphesis," 2013). However, other translations of the Bible in English, such as the Revised Standard Version, consistently render *aphesis* as "forgiveness," as does the Spanish-language Reina Valera 1960 translation.

Some argue that, although no textual or grammatical bases exist for creating a distinction between forgiveness and remission, there are theological nuances that legitimize such a separation ("Forgiveness versus remission," 2011). This argument, however, depends entirely on the reasoning of its proponents and has no objective premise.

Interestingly, in the Septuagint (the oldest Greek translation of the Old Testament), the word *aphesis* is used to describe the "release" symbolized by the Year of Jubilee, connecting the New Testament idea of the forgiveness or release from the debt of sin to the Old Testament celebration at which debtors were released from their obligations. According to Sloan (1992, pg. 397), "the term 'release' (*aphesis*) represents the primary theological and verbal connection with the Levitical proclamation of Jubilee." Sloan goes on to assert that *aphesis* is "normally translated in the NT as 'forgiveness,'" once again underscoring the fact that distinctions between "remission" and "forgiveness" in the Biblical text are artificial.

Doctrinal dangers of creating meaning

In his hermeneutical textbook *Understanding God's Word*, Bernard (2005, pg. 41) cautions against employing *eisogesis* to interpret the Word of God. Eisogesis as defined by Bernard is "putting meaning into the text." Instead, he advises that the student of the Word use *exegesis* (bringing meaning out of the text) to determine what the text says and what the authors intended to communicate to the original audience. Clearly, the writers of Scripture who consistently used *aphesis* in their writing intended to convey a single and cohesive theology of the forgiveness or remission of sin. Had they intended to create a distinction in operations, they would have used distinct words in the original language. Instead, they used a word that would have consistently conveyed a similar meaning to the original audience, who would not have had to deal with the questions created by the choice of the English translators to render *aphesis* as "remission" in some instances and "forgiveness" in others.

Forster (2010, pg. 30) correctly observes that "the dangers of eisogesis are familiar to anyone who has studied the history of biblical interpretation," adding that "countless errors and absurdities have resulted from people's determination to find in the text of the Bible a teaching that they are sure it must contain." This is abundantly true of the argument that there is a Scriptural distinction between remission and forgiveness as relates to baptism.

By adding artificial nuances to these terms and insisting they mean different things, we may unwittingly undermine the importance of one or another element of the New Birth experience. The Bible speaks of one new birth consisting of water and of the Spirit (John 3:3, 5); the Apostle Paul describes the Gospel as the death, burial, resurrection and appearing of the Lord Jesus Christ; and the Apostle Peter unites the two concepts by commanding his audience to repent (death), be baptized in the name of Jesus Christ for the *aphesis* of sins (burial/birth of water), receive the gift of the Holy Ghost (resurrection/birth of the Spirit), and save themselves from the present wicked generation (a lifestyle of holiness, or Christ appearing to the world through us) (Acts 2:38-40). If one is to contend that the unconverted sinner's sins are forgiven at the moment of repentance (a conclusion that can only be reached by taking elements of the Epistles, or Pastoral Letters, such as I John 1:8, out of context), this weakens the essentiality of water baptism by essentially stripping it of its biblical purpose, which Peter declared in Acts 2:38 to be for the *aphesis* (forgiveness) of sins.

To further illustrate, let us consider the implications of the teaching that sins are *forgiven* (the debt cancelled) at repentance and *remitted* (sent away) at baptism. While this seems on the surface to be an easy solution to the remission/forgiveness conundrum, in reality it creates more questions than answers. Firstly, repentance is not a divine action; it is a human response to a divine imperative. The word rendered "repent" in Acts 2:38 is the Greek *metanoeo*, which literally means "to change one's mind, i.e. to repent" and "to change one's mind for better, heartily to amend with abhorrence of one's past sins" ("Metanoeo," 2013). Therefore, the word "repentance" refers to the actions taken by a sinner to amend his ways; it is a change of attitude and direction. When a sinner repents, he ceases to disagree with God and begins instead to agree with Him. But this does not imply his sins are forgiven or covered; he has merely ceased to struggle against God and has admitted his culpability. The *aphesis*, or cancellation of his sin, does not occur until he submits to water baptism in the Name of Jesus Christ.

    F. F. Bruce (1952, pg. 97) describes *metanoeo* this way: "Repentance (*metanoia*, 'change of mind') involves a turning with contrition from sin to God; the repentant sinner is in the proper condition to accept the divine forgiveness." Note that repentance has not appropriated the divine forgiveness; it has merely prepared the sinner to accept it. According to the Apostle Peter, the divine forgiveness (*aphesis*) occurs at the moment of water baptism in Jesus' Name (Acts 2:38).

    We must, of necessity, also deal with a question that is so fundamental as to seem absurd, yet its validity is legitimate: what exactly does a forgiven but unremitted sin look like? If at repentance sins are forgiven, and the function of water baptism is to remit or send away those forgiven sins, what is the condition of the sinner's heart in the interim? If their sins are forgiven, do they still have effect? If not, why do they need to be washed away? And if they do, were they truly forgiven in the first place?

In the long term, holding to a false distinction between forgiveness and remission can relegate water baptism to the status of a mere ceremonial ritual, devoid of any influence on the acceptability of the repentant sinner to God because his sins are presumed to already be forgiven. This is already the case with the fundamental doctrines of an alarming number of nominally Christian or evangelical churches. The most tragic consequence of this doctrinal degeneration is that eternal souls will, on Judgment Day, learn the devastating truth that their sins were never pardoned because they omitted the critical step of water baptism.

There is danger in overcorrection as well. We can be guilty of creating such a sharp distinction between repentance and water baptism that we fail to acknowledge the role of each in the process of forgiveness or remission of sins. Peter established both as critical to *aphesis*. The fact is, a heart that has not undergone *metanoeo* is unprepared for *aphesis*; in order for sins to be forgiven at baptism, baptism must be preceded by thorough and genuine repentance. The absence of either element will render the process of conversion void and will prevent *aphesis* from occurring.

Conclusion

Although the existence of a distinction between remission and forgiveness of sins in the biblical context has long been debated among Apostolics, a careful study of the Scriptures using sound hermeneutical practices and appeals to the original languages dispels the idea of such a distinction. Instead, the Scripture reveals through the consistent use of *aphesis* that remission and forgiveness of sins are synonymous terms. This is further confirmed by the fact that many reputable and reliable translations of the Bible make no distinction between the terms, consistently rendering *aphesis* as "forgiveness."

The danger of using eisogesis or inserting meaning into the biblical text is that we can undermine the essentiality of critical elements of the salvation message. Repentance is where the sinner prepares his heart for forgiveness, while water baptism is where divine forgiveness is applied to the prepared heart. It is not proper, however, to so sharply distinguish between the two that the critical role of either is omitted from the process of *aphesis*.

References

Aphesis. (2013). Retrieved October 13, 2013, from http://www.blueletterbible.org/lang/lexicon/lexicon.cfm?Strongs=G859&t=KJV

Assemblies of God fundamental truths. (2010, March 1). Retrieved October 13, 2013, from http://ag.org/top/Beliefs/Statement_of_Fundamental_Truths/sft_short.cfm

Bernard, D. (2005). *Understanding God's Word*. (p. 41). Hazelwood, MO: Word Aflame Press.

Bruce, F. F. 1952. *The Acts of the Apostles*. (p. 97). London: Tyndale.

Forgive. (2013). Retrieved October 13, 2013, from http://www.merriam-webster.com/dictionary/forgive

Forgiveness versus remission of sins. (2011, October 9). Retrieved October 13, 2013, from http://rationalityoffaith.wordpress.com/2011/10/09/forgiveness-versus-remission-of-sins/

Forster, G. (2010). *The contested public square: the crisis of Christianity and politics*. (p. 30). Downers Grove, IL: InterVarsity Press.

Metanoeo. (2013). Retrieved October 14, 2013, from http://www.blueletterbible.org/lang/lexicon/lexicon.cfm?Strongs=G3340&t=KJV

Remit. (2013). Retrieved October 13, 2013, from http://www.merriam-webster.com/dictionary/remitting?show=0&t=1381720601

Repentance. In (1985). R. M. Davis (Ed.), *Bible doctrines: Foundation of the church* (p. 68). Hazelwood, MO: Word Aflame Press.

Sloan, R. B. (1992). Jubilee. In J. Green, S. McKnight & I. H. Marshal (Eds.), *Dictionary of Jesus and the Gospels* (p. 397). Downers Grove, IL: InterVarsity Press.

What we believe. (2013). Retrieved from http://www.cogic.org/our-foundation/what-we-believe/

Appendix B

To Baptize, or Not to Baptize? Dealing With the Issue of Cohabitation

Kelly Nix

Due to the increasing number of couples in our society who are living together without the benefit of marriage, we are encountering more and more frequently the difficulty that arises when one or both "companions" in a live-in situation request water baptism. Sad and complicated situations that make legal marriage difficult have complicated the lives of many who later begin to try to get their lives right with God. In the following essay, we will attempt to examine this sensitive situation by the light of the Scriptures, while bearing in mind that, even though society often changes its standards, God and His Word are eternally immutable. Let us consider, then, some of the more popular arguments in favor of baptizing people who are not legally married:

"If God gave the Holy Ghost, who am I to deny water baptism?"

There are pastors who ask, "If God fills someone with the Holy Ghost, who am I to deny water baptism?" On the surface, this argument would seem to have some merit. Nonetheless, upon closer examination, it is not valid. In the first place, one of the Biblical prerequisites for baptism is repentance, or the act of abandoning ones sins. Without a doubt, no truly Apostolic pastor would deny this fact. The most famous baptizer of the Bible, John the Baptist, did not baptize just anybody without first considering their moral situation. His standard was, "**Bring forth therefore fruits meet for repentance**: and think not to say within yourselves, We have Abraham to our father: for I say unto you, that God is able of these stones to raise up children unto Abraham. And now also the axe is laid unto the root of the trees: therefore every tree which bringeth not forth good fruit is hewn down, and cast into the fire" (Matthew 3:8-10).

How can it be right to deny baptism to those who have already received the Holy Ghost? God gives the Holy Ghost on the basis of faith and repentance. It is very important to note that God's function in giving the Holy Ghost is very different from the pastor's function in administering water baptism. God, who has the power to look into the future, does not permit Himself to exercise that power in the case of a sinner. Were it so, He would never give the Holy Ghost to someone who later would backslide. In certain cases, He accepts by faith the sinner's promise to leave his sins, as soon as he so promises, and rewards his faith by filling him with the Holy Ghost. Remember, the Holy Ghost is a gift from God. We know that it is possible to grieve the Holy Ghost until He withdraws from the life of a person who insists in continuing in sin. If God consented to live in that person, He can also make the decision to cease doing so should they not follow through on their promise and obey His Word. This is not the case with water baptism: water baptism is a sacrament that is administered by man, and that cannot be taken away. Once a person has been baptized, they remain baptized. The precious name of Jesus Christ is permanently connected to that person, in spite of his/her sinful actions, thus bringing great shame and reproach upon the name of Jesus.

John the Baptist demanded proof of repentance before baptizing a candidate. He demanded "fruits meet for repentance." In the case of someone who is cohabiting outside of marriage, which is fornication, or, in certain cases, adultery (in the case of one or both partners being married to someone else), the "fruits meet for repentance" could be expressed in one of two ways: 1) by legalizing the marriage, or 2) by terminating the immoral relationship.

When Jesus healed the sick man, He admonished him, "Behold, thou art made whole: sin no more, lest a worse thing come unto thee" (John 5:14). Someone who baptizes a person who is living in sin, knowing that that person will get out of the baptistry and go right back to a situation of fornication or adultery, runs the risk of condemning that person to a worse fate. This is a very serious responsibility.

Some will say, "But, if that person dies before they are able to straighten out their situation, and they were not baptized due to my refusal to baptize them, then I will be responsible for their soul." This is not the case! Were it so, John would never have placed conditions on baptism. If the individual is not willing to abandon sin (leave the immoral situation or legalize the marriage), he/she did not have a genuine repentance experience. Therefore, baptism would not help them anyway. Remember, if you baptize a person who intends to keep living in sin, you are endorsing their sin. Don't be guilty of this! Jesus came to save the world **FROM** their sins, not **IN** their sins (Matthew 1:20).

As we have already mentioned, fornication and adultery are horrible sins, the same as other types of sexual immorality. When a man begins to live in a sexual relationship with a woman without legal marriage, their first sexual act is fornication , or adultery, if one or both of them have another legal marriage partner. Each subsequent sexual act between them is a new instance of adultery or fornication. We ask, does the act of fathering a family in a situation of adultery or fornication cause those sins to cease to be sin? Of course not! Notwithstanding, the idea exists amongst some in the church that we have no right to condemn those who have families that are a product of adultery or fornication. Brethren, those families never had a right to exist, in God's eyes! Is it sad? Yes! Is it a difficult situation? Yes! But that doesn't change the Word of God! If those individuals truly want to make things right with God, they must face reality: they were the ones who entered into that immoral situation, and they are the ones who will have to straighten it out. It was not God's fault that they decided to ignore the laws governing marriage. We must reach a decision: do we believe the Word of God just as it is written, or only in situations where it is easy to do so?

The Word of God states clearly that the sexually immoral will not inherit the kingdom of God, but will have their part in the lake of fire (Ephesians 5:5-6; Revelation 21:8). What will God's opinion be of us if we try to introduce or endorse immoral situations in the kingdom, legitimizing people who are openly and flagrantly practicing sexual sins, without considering the severe condemnation the Word of God expresses of those sins? Why should the alcoholic have to leave his liquor, the drug addict have to leave his drugs, the thief have to stop stealing, yet some fornicators and adulterers not have to leave their immorality simply because, in the course of their sinful acts, they created families? Does the act of creating a family make sin to not be sin, make adultery cease being adultery, and fornication stop being fornication? The man who has an illegitimate family has a responsibility to continue to provide for it, but should find another place to live until he finds a legal and moral solution for his marriage. Only then can he be legitimately baptized.

It is absurd to say that, if we practice it long enough, sin will cease to be sin. After 20 years of thievery, a thief is still a thief. After 20 years of drinking, a drunk is still a drunk. And, after 20 years of committing adultery, and adulterer is still an adulterer. If the drunkard should say, "Pastor, I want to be baptized, and then I want to go home and have a beer," would it be right for the pastor to baptize him? Of course not! He would not be showing fruits of true repentance. By the same token, it is wrong to baptize a person knowing that he/she will return home to commit another act of adultery or fornication. That person is not demonstrating true repentance.

"Let every man abide in the same calling wherein he was called" (I Corinthians 7:17-24)

Another popular argument is drawn from I Corinthians 7:17-24, where it says, "...let every man, wherein he is called, therein abide with God." To quote the old saying, "A text without a context is a pretext." It is essential to take each scripture in its context, that is, in light of the verses immediately preceding and following. The context of this scripture deals exclusively with legal and legitimate marriage. It speaks of a person who is married to an unbeliever. If the legal marriage partner, even being an unbeliever, agrees to continue living peacefully with the believer, the believer must not seek to change his/her marital status. By no means is this speaking of "live-ins," people who through their actions make a mockery of the holy state of matrimony established by God. If we are to apply this passage to "live-ins," then we must also apply it to murderers, thieves, drunkards, etc. In that case, no one would have to change their lives or abandon sin in order to be a Christian. This argument does not make sense.

The passage uses as examples slaves, freemen, circumcised, and uncircumcised. All of those conditions were legal and legitimate, and not immoral like adultery. It is extremely inappropriate to attempt to use this passage to justify baptizing people who are living in sexual immorality.

"The pastor has authority to retain or to forgive sin" (John 20:23)

Be very careful with trying to use this passage to justify baptizing "live-ins." Even though this passage clearly refers to baptism, and the only power a minister has to forgive sins is through administering water baptism in the name of Jesus Christ (Acts 2:38), do not forget that Acts 2:38 also establishes repentance as a prerequisite for baptism. **A repented sin is an abandoned sin**. The same verse that authorizes the pastor to remit, absolve, or forgive sin also gives him the right to retain that sin. God will in no way look unfavorably on a pastor who refuses baptism on the basis of a lack of repentance. On the other hand, God will most certainly judge someone who tries to legitimize, through baptism, something God hates, abhors, and unequivocally condemns.

"Inside the church, the pastor gives the orders, not the law"

While some have actually used this argument to justify baptizing "live-ins," this is a very dangerous and unbiblical position. Romans 13:1-5 says, "Let every soul be subject unto the higher powers. For there is no power but of God: the powers that be are ordained of God. Whosoever therefore resisteth the power, resisteth the ordinance of God: and they that resist shall receive to themselves damnation. For rulers are not a terror to good works, but to the evil. Wilt thou then not be afraid of the power? do that which is good, and thou shalt have praise of the same: For he is the minister of God to thee for good. But if thou do that which is evil, be afraid; for he beareth not the sword in vain: for he is the minister of God, a revenger to execute wrath upon him that doeth evil. Wherefore ye must needs be subject, not only for wrath, but also for conscience sake."

If a nation's laws are immoral and are contrary to the Word of God, then the Bible clearly has supremacy; however, the laws requiring legal marriage do not contradict the Word of God – instead, they complement it. Therefore, we are Biblically, civilly, morally, and ethically obligated to observe them.

Made in the USA
Columbia, SC
15 March 2021